G is for Gladiator

An Ancient Rome Alphabet

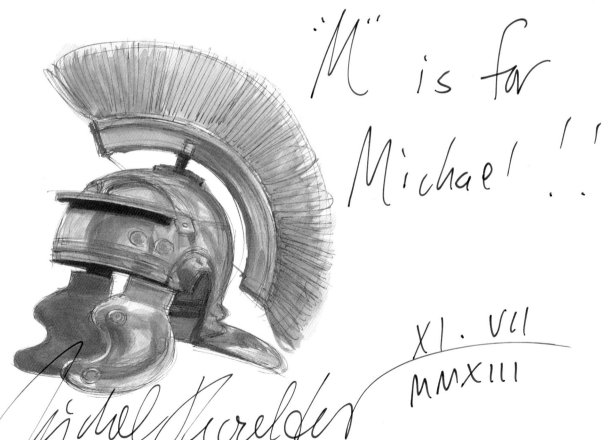

"M" is for Michael!!

XI. VII
MMXIII

Written by Debbie and Michael Shoulders and Illustrated by Victor Juhasz

To all of the ancient peoples of Italia who are part of my heritage,
especially my grandparents, John and Carmela Cacicia

D. S.

∽

To my Italian mother-in-law, Mary Jane Cacicia Adams

M. S.

∽

For Magnus Xander Juhasz

V. J.

Text Copyright © 2010 Debbie and Michael Shoulders
Illustration Copyright © 2010 Victor Juhasz

Sleeping Bear Press™
315 E. Eisenhower Parkway, Suite 200
Ann Arbor MI 48103
www.sleepingbearpress.com

© 2010 Sleeping Bear Press is an imprint of Gale, a part of Cengage Learning.

Printed and bound in the United States.

10 9 8 7 6 5 4 3 2 1

Library of Congress Cataloging-in-Publication Data

Shoulders, Debbie.
G is for gladiator : an ancient Rome alphabet / written by Debbie and
Michael Shoulders ; illustrated by Victor Juhasz. —1st ed.
p. cm.
ISBN 978-1-58536-457-2
1. Rome — History — Juvenile literature. 2. Rome — Social life and
customs — Juvenile literature. 3. Alphabet books — Juvenile literature.
I. Shoulders, Michael. II. Juhasz, Victor, ill. III. Title.
DG77.S488 2010
937— dc22   2009037414

The Roman Empire
at its peak, around AD 117

CALEDONIA
(Scotland)

HIBERNIA
(Ireland)

Hadrian's Wall

BRITTANIA
(Britain)

London

ATLANTIC OCEAN

GERMANIA
INFERIOR
(Belgium/Netherlands)

GERMANIA MAGNA
(Germany)

GERMANIA
SUPERIOR
*(Portions of W. Switzerland
W. Germany, Alsace)*

GALLIA
(France)

DACIA

Black Sea

ILLYRIA

Caspian Sea

ARMENIA

ITALIA *(Italy)*

Cosica

HISPANIA
(Spain)

(The Balkan Countries)

Byzantium

Rome

THRACIA

PARTHIA
(Northeastern Iran)

MACEDONIA

Sardinia

GREECE

ASIA MINOR
(Turkey)

Siclily

Athens

MESOPOTAMIA
(Iraq)

Carthage

NUMIDIA
(Algeria, Tunisia)

Cyprus

SYRIA

NORTH AFRICA

Mediterranean Sea

Crete

Jerusalem

ARABIA

Alexandria

CYRENAICA
(Libya)

AEGYPTUS
(Egypt)

Red Sea

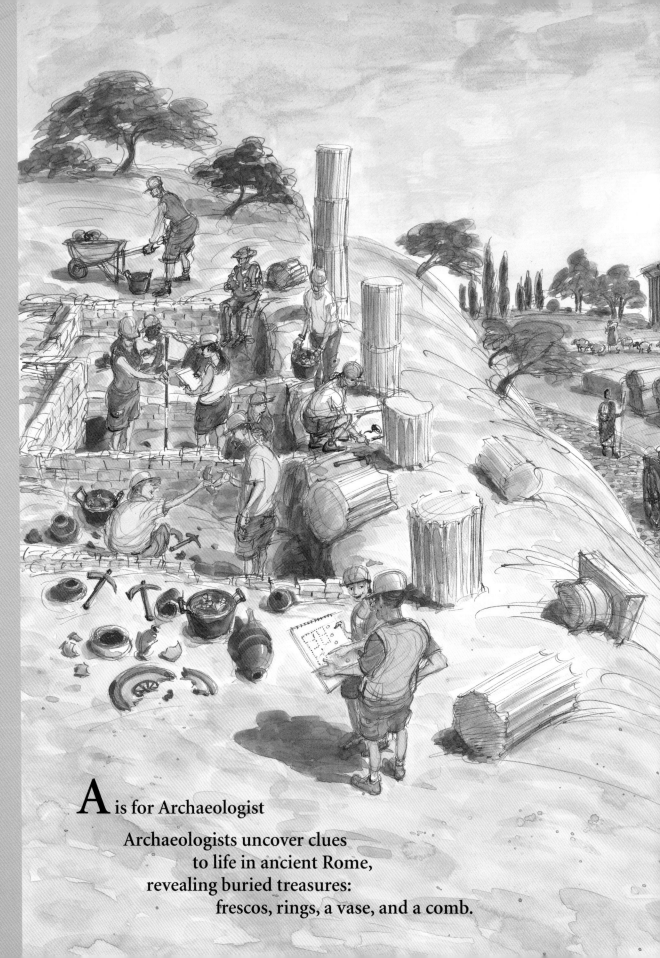

The story of Rome began in 753 BC. Rome is called the "Eternal City" because its citizens developed language, art, and technology that still exists. The many archaeological ruins found in Italy today continue to share information of a sophisticated culture founded thousands of years ago. The chipped stone columns of the Roman Forum talk of architectural styles and the kind of technology that was used to erect the temples and basilicas. Bronze etchings and stone carvings show how the people looked and dressed. The Romans were the first civilization to accurately model the human body through sculpture. They left portraits of their leaders and important members of society. Even tombstones hold writings that give information about the daily lives and culture of the people.

As early as 1450, archaeologists began to collect the utensils, tools, and coins that provided clues to early Roman culture. Today, plans for additional subway tracks and new highways needed to transport Rome's 2.8 million inhabitants are constantly revised as archaeological digs recover artifacts that tell new stories of Rome's glory days.

A is for Archaeologist

Archaeologists uncover clues
to life in ancient Rome,
revealing buried treasures:
frescos, rings, a vase, and a comb.

B is for Building

Many ancient buildings
still stand today in Rome:
bridges, temples, statues, and
Pantheon's massive dome.

Roman engineers were leaders in the use of cement, baked brick, arches, and domes. They were so successful that many of their buildings still stand. Visitors can walk the Appian Way, an ancient highway stretching from Rome to the present-day city of Brindisi on the coast of the Adriatic Sea, a distance of 363 miles (584 km).

The building of roads was important in helping to connect the various cultures of the Empire. This could not have been done without a large supply of slaves and soldiers. Slaves were people who had been stripped of their freedom, often captured when Rome acquired new territories or bought from slave traders. They worked to construct a network of 53,000 miles (85,000 km) of highways. A surveyor located the flattest and most direct route. Then workers cleared brush and earth to dig a trench 3½ feet (1 m) deep. The trench was filled with layers of sand, concrete, and stones. The workers then placed a curved surface, or camber, over the stones and dug side ditches to steer water away and prevent cracking. This method was so effective that these ancient paths were used well into modern times. Today asphalt is placed over the old road to build up the surface.

Bb

Breaking the law in ancient Rome had consequences, just like today. The Romans recorded their laws on the Twelve Tables published in 450 BC. They were organized in twelve sections and displayed for all citizens in the Roman Forum, describing laws about money, marriage, property rights, inheritance, and public behavior. For example, one such law stated that if a neighbor's tree bent by the wind fell over to your farm, you could petition for its removal. The legal system evolved and changed but it was always based on the Twelve Tables.

Unlike our system today, an individual initiated court action rather than the court system. If individuals felt they had been wronged, they would consult a *praetor*, an elected magistrate, similar to a lawyer today, who would decide if a trial was needed. The praetor would then seek a judge to oversee the proceedings. The offended person also had to make sure the accused was present in court, even using force if necessary.

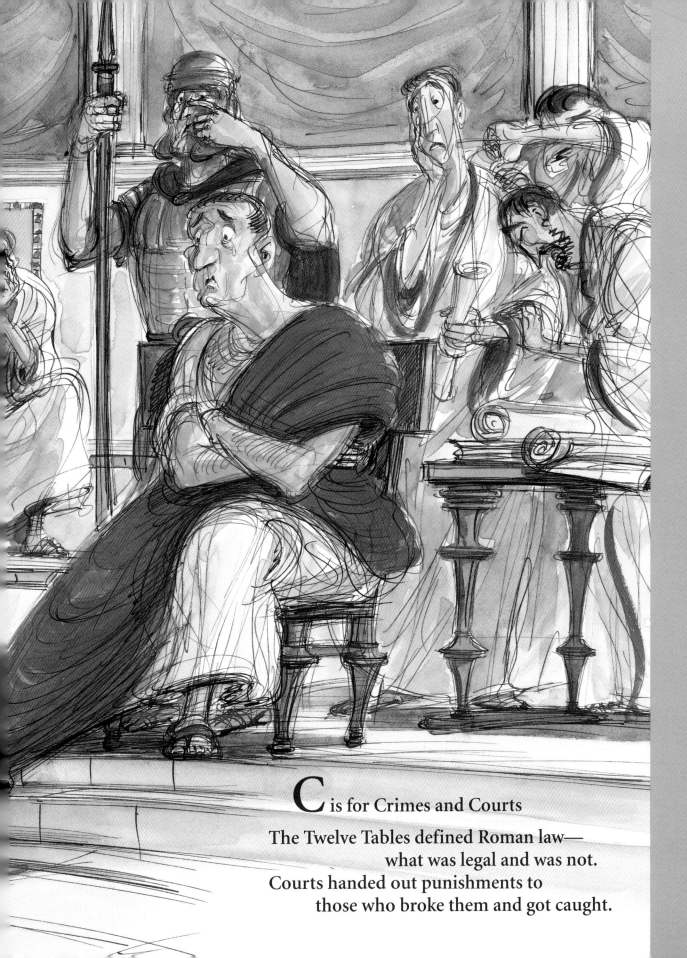

If the case was scandalous enough, the trial might be conducted in a larger forum like a basilica. This made room for spectators to cheer and jeer the proceedings, perhaps influencing the outcome. Defendants might come to court dressed in rags with ashes covering their hair. A weeping spouse would complete the picture, all designed to arouse sympathy from the crowd. In important cases, a jury of up to seventy-five people voted and decided the outcome, while the judge administered punishment. A guilty person could be exiled to a distant land in the Roman Empire, lose their citizenship or property, or be included in the gladiator games.

C is for Crimes and Courts

The Twelve Tables defined Roman law—
what was legal and was not.
Courts handed out punishments to
those who broke them and got caught.

Burial traditions depended on beliefs of the afterlife. Most Romans thought that after a person died their spirit crossed a river (the Styx) to the underworld (Hades). The corpse was prepared for such a journey. Some even put coins under the tongue of the dead to pay for the ferry ride to Hades. It was believed that after judgment in Hades, the spirit would be sent to heaven (Elysium) or hell (Tartarus).

When an important person died, the body was bathed and covered with oils in preparation for a laying out in the atrium of the home. The body was displayed with candles and wreathes, and visitors came to pay respects. At the time of the funeral, held at night, eight men carried the body to the Forum to give speeches of praise for the deceased. The dead were buried in a stone or marble coffin.

Since it was against the law to bury people in the city limits, the main roads outside of Rome were covered with monuments to the dead. These stone tributes were engraved with scenes of daily life, a useful cultural artifact. Some of them still stand today.

Dd

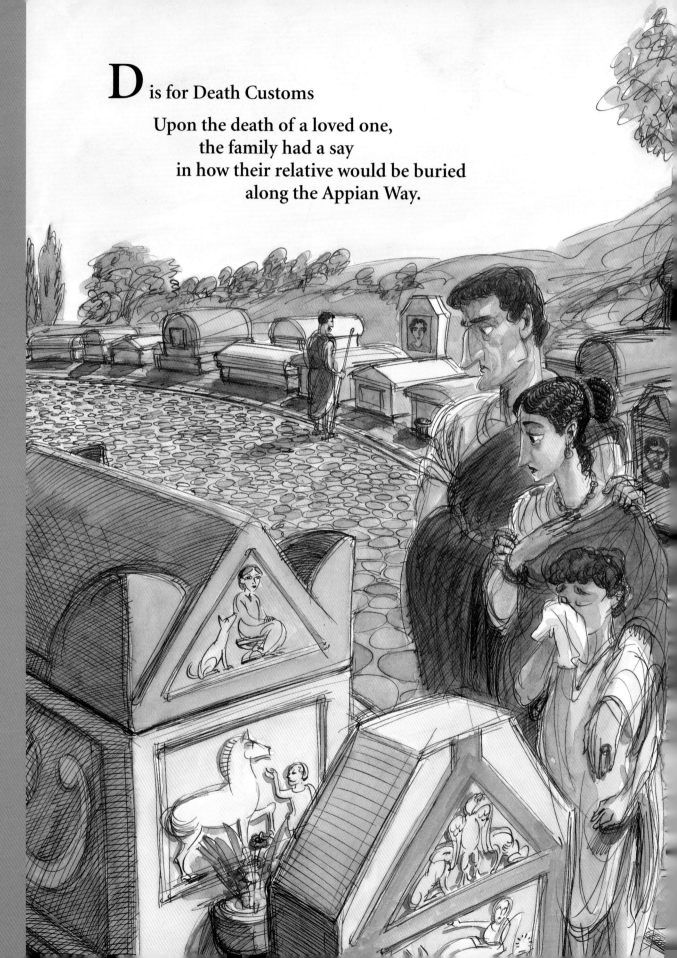

D is for Death Customs

Upon the death of a loved one,
the family had a say
in how their relative would be buried
along the Appian Way.

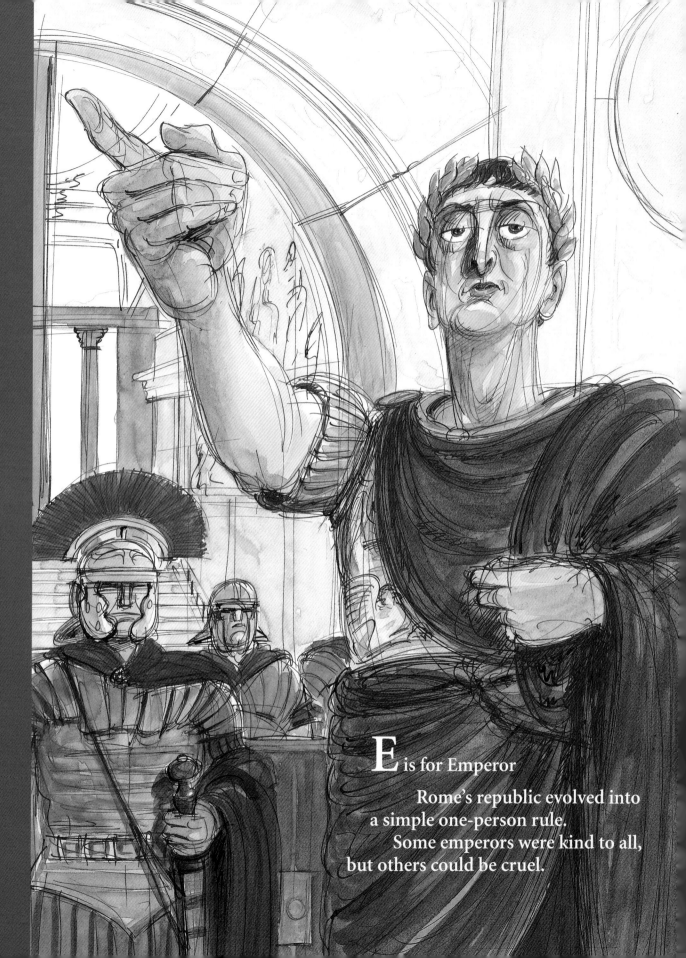

Civil wars and individual fights for power brought an end to the Republic, which was ruled by elected citizens. The Roman Empire rose in its place, and began with a succession of 147 emperors, reigning from 27 BC until AD 476. Some of them brought greatness to Rome while others were more interested in their own selfish desires, leaving Rome's citizens to fend for themselves.

The first emperor, Octavius (63 BC to AD 14), was the grandnephew and adopted son of Julius Caesar, the last dictator of the Roman Republic. At Caesar's death, Octavius joined forces with Marc Antony to seek revenge on Caesar's assassins but the two men were not close. Octavius preferred living in Rome while Marc Antony went to Northern Africa and soon they began fighting. Their relationship ended in a naval battle off the coast of Greece with Octavius commanding the winning fleet.

Working with the consul and senate, Octavius was renamed Augustus, meaning "the exalted." He was declared the emperor of the Roman Empire. Augustus built roads and bridges to connect the provinces and put governors in charge of each. Interested in culture, he constructed temples and encouraged writing and music, all helping to beautify Rome.

E is for Emperor

Rome's republic evolved into
a simple one-person rule.
Some emperors were kind to all,
but others could be cruel.

F is for Festivals

Romans attended festivals
held throughout the year.
They loved the chariot races,
and were always ready to cheer.

Ff

More than one hundred festivals brought families and friends together to honor Roman gods, the seasons, and family members. Some examples include the *Parentalia*, which was an occasion to remember dead parents with gifts of flowers, milk, and wine. It was believed that these items helped the spirit to move on and not haunt the living. The plebeians, or common Roman citizens, recognized *Anna Perenna*, the goddess of the new year, in March with picnics along the Tiber River. The people drank wine believing that every cup predicted how many years one would live.

A two-week festival, the *Ludi Romani*, paid homage to Jupiter, the king of all Roman gods. It began on September 5th and was highlighted by races and visits to the theater. Most towns had a track for chariot races. The *Circus Maximus* in Rome held 250,000 spectators. People placed bets on which charioteer would win. This helped the charioteers gain fame although the efforts could be dangerous. It was common for chariots to ram each other causing overturns with injuries or death.

Outdoor theaters held up to seven thousand people. Theatergoers sat on stone seats in a semicircle around the stage. The actors had to wear masks so that they could be seen at a distance. The mask signified an emotion like happy or sad.

Gg

Early Romans enjoyed a good fight—as spectators. The Colosseum was begun in AD 75 by Emperor Vespasian and completed by his son, Emperor Titus, in AD 80 as a gift for the people. The stadium was 160 feet (48 m) high and held 50,000 seated spectators.

A full day of free entertainment began with a procession of dancers, jugglers, and musicians in front of the emperor. Next came a parade of rare beasts such as bears or panthers. These animals might appear later in the arena as a gladiator's opponent. The last and most anticipated event was the gladiator fight.

Gladiators, usually slaves or convicted criminals between sixteen and twenty-four years old, fought with few weapons, sometimes until death. It is a popular opinion that gladiators always fought to the death, but this wasn't the case. It would have been a waste of training! Gladiators trained for up to two years. These men, and occasionally women, were the superstars of the era. They signed playbills before the shows and might even wear advertisements endorsing local businesses.

The victor received a palm branch, a crown, money, and sometimes, freedom. Should the fight end in a draw, the crowd might be asked to show mercy.

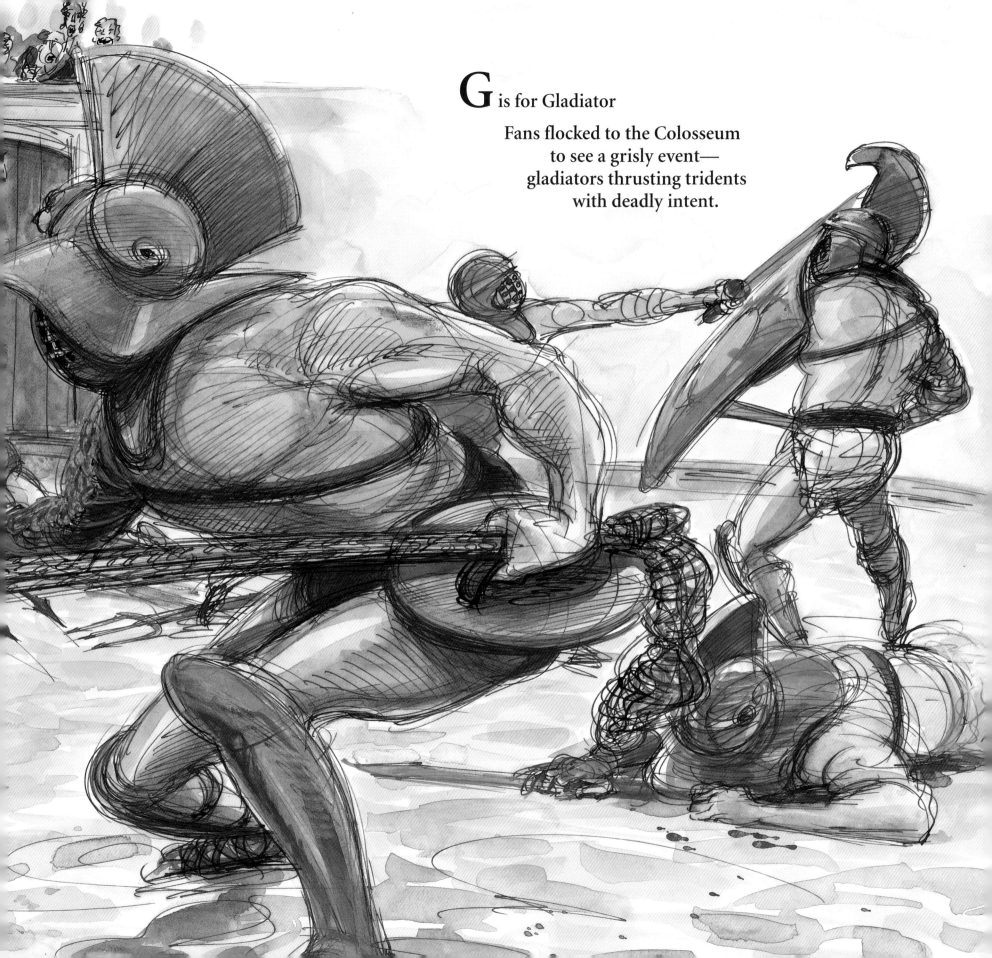

G is for Gladiator

Fans flocked to the Colosseum
to see a grisly event—
gladiators thrusting tridents
with deadly intent.

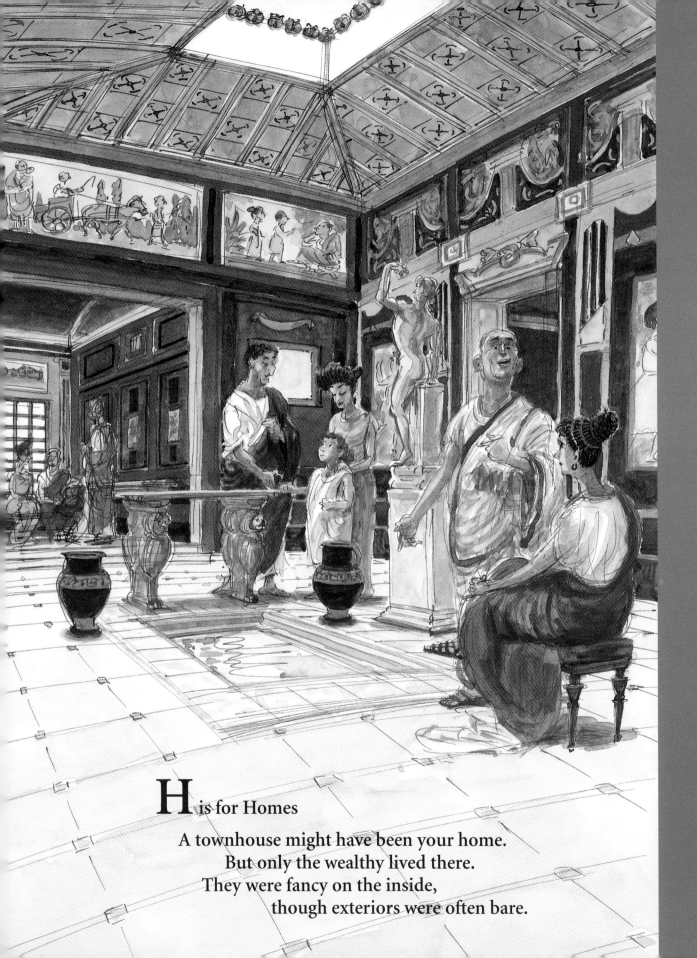

Wealthy citizens lived in townhouses (*domus*). The less fortunate lived in apartments (*insulae*). Owners kept the exterior of a domus plain to discourage robbers. The rooms were built around a roofless courtyard. The family captured rain in a basin or ornamental pool (*impluvium*). Visitors might gather in the living room (*tablinum*). The walls were covered with frescos, paintings created on wet plaster that depicted Roman life. From the frescos, archaeologists learned that furniture was made from wood and lamps were made from olive oil or candle reeds dipped in wax.

Most people lived in apartments. These could be quite lovely or downright awful. Usually four or five floors tall, the bottom part was built with stone. The upper floors were constructed with wood and were usually the homes for poor tenants. The rooms were heated with wood-burning braziers, which meant fires were prevalent. There were no stoves so people ate their food raw or bought it already cooked. They gathered water from public fountains and threw waste out onto the street.

H is for Homes

A townhouse might have been your home.
But only the wealthy lived there.
They were fancy on the inside,
though exteriors were often bare.

I is for Italy

Italy has many tales to tell
of its ancient history.
Stories of Romulus and Remus
are part of Roman mythology.

I i

Early Romans taught their children the legend of Romulus and Remus. It was said that as babies the twin boys were thrown into the Tiber River by a jealous uncle but later rescued and raised by a she-wolf. Wanting to build a city on the land of their rescue, the brothers fought over dividing lines and Romulus killed Remus. In 753 BC Rome began and Romulus was declared the first king. The legend has some basis in fact according to archaeological finds. Visitors to Rome can view the site of Romulus's hut on the Palatine Hill.

Through defense of territory and changes in leaders and governments, the Roman Empire grew, taking in most of the lands surrounding the Mediterranean Sea. This time of cultural, economic, and political growth continued until AD 200. At that point invading tribes attacked. Higher taxes were needed to finance the military and protect the people. Citizens complained and the military was divided in their support of various leaders. Poor leadership from the emperors and chaos brought an end to Rome's glory. The Goths, a Germanic tribe, conquered the Romans in AD 476.

The Roman Catholic pope was put in charge of Rome in AD 540, and the land was divided into Papal States, territories ruled by the pope. In 1861 the provinces became nationalized as a kingdom under the name of Italy, ruled by King Victor Emmanuel II.

J j

J is for Jupiter and Juno

Romans tried not to anger the gods,
for some could be quite frightening.
If Jupiter got cross, beware—
a mighty bolt of lightning!

The Romans believed powerful gods controlled all aspects of their lives, from Jupiter, the god of all gods to Robigus, the god of mildew! Keeping the gods happy ensured good fortune. When lied to, Jupiter might retaliate with vicious lightning bolts.

The Romans merged their beliefs with the conquered civilizations that became part of their growing empire. The Greek culture was especially interwoven, with Jupiter inheriting many of the traits of the Greek god Zeus. When the Egyptian Queen Cleopatra visited Rome, she brought with her the promise of an afterlife in the worship of the goddess Isis. Soldiers turned to the Persian god Mithras for courage. The Romans did not force their own gods on the conquered peoples, but interest in new rituals often brought about a blending of cultures.

Romans constantly looked for signs of a pleased or unhappy god. An *augur* (priest) would examine the liver of a sacrificed animal for signs of disease. They also might feed sacred chickens. If the animals did not eat then the god was certainly angry and had to be pleased!

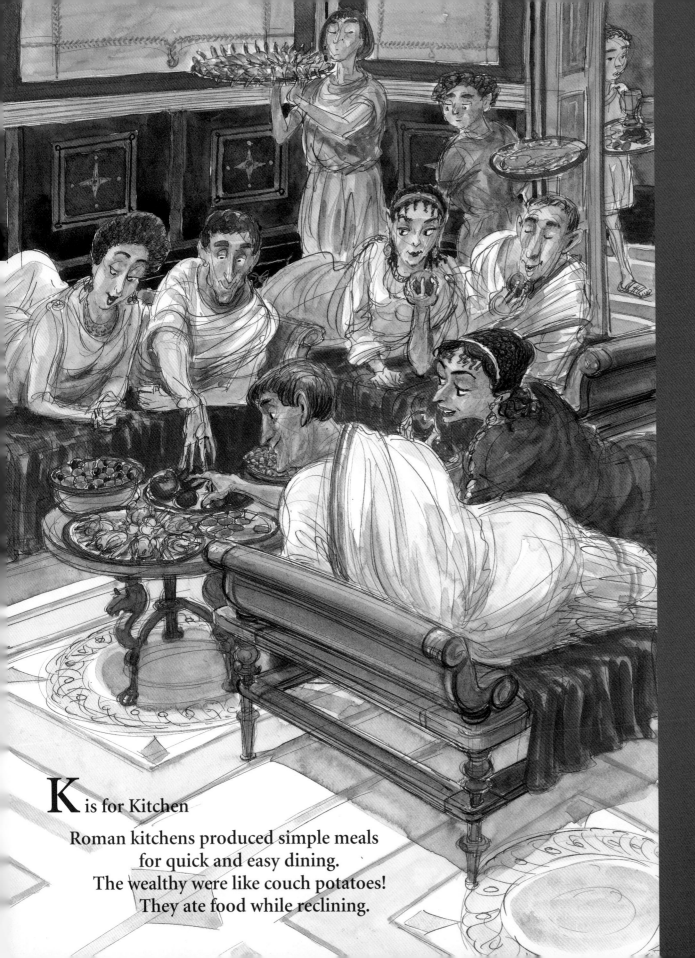

K is for Kitchen

Roman kitchens produced simple meals
for quick and easy dining.
The wealthy were like couch potatoes!
They ate food while reclining.

Mosaics, images made from small pieces of glass or stone, teach us that Romans ate simple foods. Breakfast was olives, figs, honey, and porridge or bread made from wheat and lunch might include bread and cheese. Dinner might be a soup of turnips, onions, and beans. The diet evolved into something richer as Roman territories expanded to include foods from other cultures.

Poor families cooked on the street or borrowed a baker's oven. Slaves of wealthy citizens worked in kitchens over charcoal fires on brick hearths. Meats were roasted in the ashes of fires and flavored with olive oil, vinegar, wine, and a spicy fish sauce (*liquamen* or *garum*).

Well-to-do families hosted extravagant meals. They ate their main meal (*cena*) at 4:00 after most Romans had visited the baths. The family and guests would lie on couches that surrounded three sides of the table. Slaves served food, water, and towels from the fourth side of the table. The first course was often salad, eggs, snails, or shellfish. That course concluded with *mulsum* (wine) sweetened with honey. Next came meats, fish, wild boar, or pheasant. Lucky guests might have been served dormouse (rodent) stuffed with pork and pine nuts. Finally, a dessert cake or fruit was served.

L is for Legion

Marius formed a legion
to defend all Rome's frontier.
Each legionary was issued
a dagger, shield, and spear.

The first Roman army helped the city only in times of need. Soldiers protected Roman territories. When those talents were not needed, they built roads and bridges. To prepare for their tough job, small disciplined groups trained with weapons and long marches.

In 107 BC, Marius, a military commander and consul of the Republic, built an organized and disciplined army. He divided it into groups called legions. Each legion had 5,500 men (legionaries), was numbered, and given a nickname and a silver eagle (*aquila*). If an enemy captured the aquila, the legion disbanded.

Anyone could join the army. Most men stayed for up to twenty-five years. Each man received the same weapons: a dagger, a long spear, and a leather shield. The men wore uniforms of overlapping plates of armor (*cuirass*). These durable metals are archaeological clues to the past. Soldiers paid for their protective garments using their monthly wage of 225–300 *denarii*, Roman money, or supplied their own if they were too poor to afford it.

Ll

Roman couples entered into marriage at a young age. Girls married by fourteen; boys a little older. The girl's father arranged the marriage, considering what was best for the family. A marriage contract was discussed at an engagement ceremony (*sponsalia*) and the bride-to-be placed a ring on the third finger of her left hand. It was important to choose the perfect wedding date. Late June was considered lucky.

The bride's house was festooned with flowers and ribbons, and the bride wore a white tunic and a headdress of flowers covering a red veil. The marriage contract was signed and the bride promised, "Whichever family you belong to, I also belong," and, "Where you are master, I am mistress."

The crowd wished the couple good luck and the bride offered her childhood toys to the household shrine. The guests enjoyed a special wedding cake that honored the gods and goddesses. The groom led his new wife home through a procession of torchlight and flutes and carried her over the threshold rather than risk any tripping.

M
m

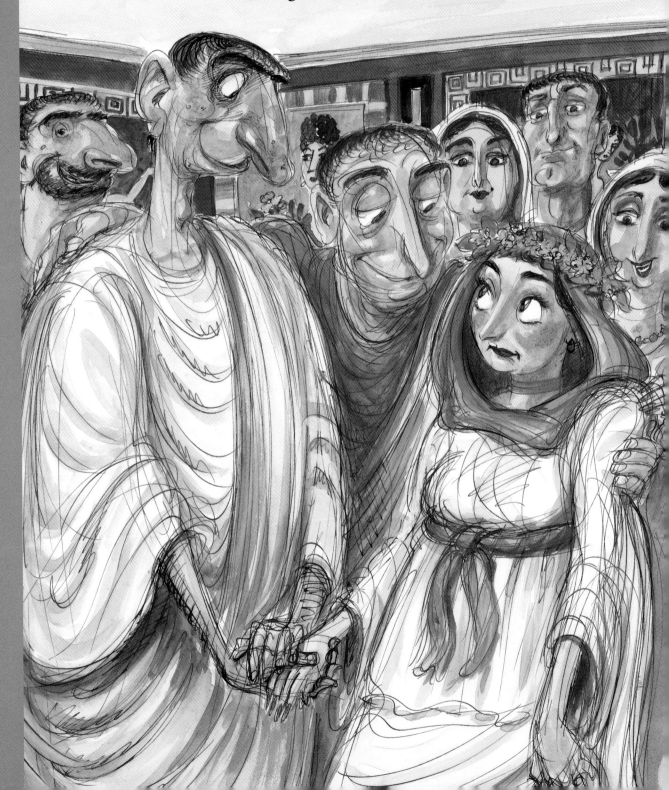

M is for Marriage

A Roman bride had no say
as to who would be her spouse.
Her father picked the man
he thought best to share her house.

N is for Naval Activities

Naval activities made Rome great.
Their ships sailed to many lands.
Exporting foods and importing goods
helped Rome's empire to expand.

Much of the Roman Empire surrounded the Mediterranean Sea. This includes modern-day Spain, France, Turkey, Northern Africa, and the Middle East. Augustus built a fleet of ships responsible for importing and exporting goods across the Empire. Exported items were the main source of food for the Roman people.

Shipwrecks, coins, engravings, and mosaics have contributed to the understanding of the Roman shipping industry. The artifacts explained where the ships traveled, how they were designed, and what cargo they held. Cargo ships were usually 50–55 feet (15–16 m) long and could move about four miles (6 km) per hour, generally traveling one hundred miles (161 km) a day. A sailing trip from Egypt to Rome would take two to three weeks.

The Romans exported sacks of grain and pottery jars (*amphorae*) filled with oil and wine, as well as silks and spices, to the vast ranges of their domain. They imported items like olive oil, fish sauces, and metals from Baetica, the Andalusia region of Spain. Ships from North Africa brought marble, corn, and purple dye.

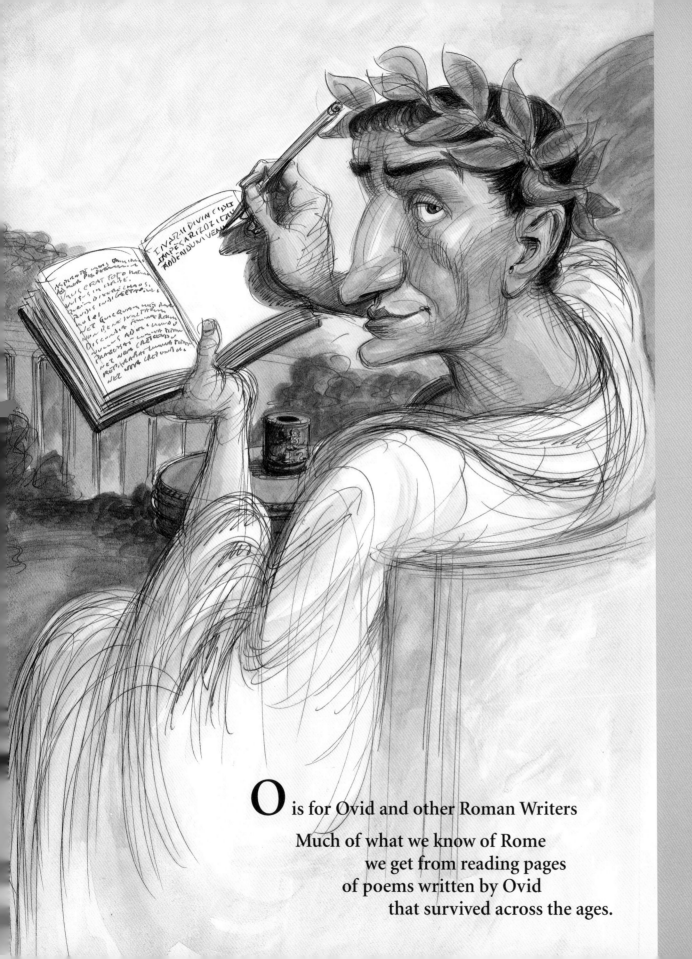

The arts took a backseat to politics and the legal system in early Roman times. Leaders like Augustus realized that writers could influence their causes. Much of what is known of ancient Roman life comes from the writings of that period.

Ovid (43 BC to AD 17) wrote descriptive poetry. His piece, *Metamorphoses*, contained fifteen books of legends and myths that emphasized change.

Virgil (70 to 19 BC) may be the best poet of the ancient period. His epic poem, *The Aeneid*, takes place before the founding of Rome. It tells of the heroic deeds of Prince Aeneas. Virgil wrote it to explain the expansion of the Roman Empire. Twelve books in all, *The Aeneid* still stands as a masterpiece of epic poetry.

Livy (59 BC to AD 17) wrote 142 books on Roman history. Some question the accuracy of this information because Livy mixed common legends with facts.

Horace (65 to 8 BC) created poetry about a society ruled by Emperor Augustus. This gave a modern-day peek into the lifestyles of the rich and famous.

Pliny the Younger (AD 62 to 113) was a letter writer. He left nine books detailing life in ancient Rome.

O is for Ovid and other Roman Writers

Much of what we know of Rome
we get from reading pages
of poems written by Ovid
that survived across the ages.

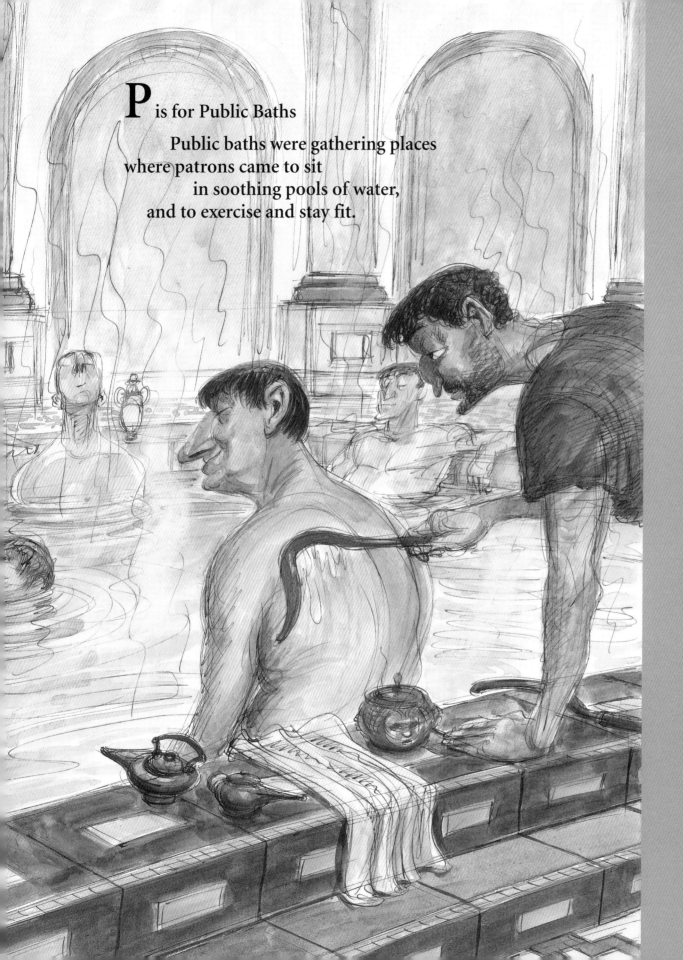

P is for Public Baths

Public baths were gathering places
where patrons came to sit
in soothing pools of water,
and to exercise and stay fit.

One way to enjoy good health was to visit one of Rome's nine hundred public baths! They were often built near water sources thought to have healing powers. For a small fee citizens could enjoy facilities that included hot and cold water, pools, exercise courtyards, and libraries. Public bathing was a time for chatting and relaxation.

Slaves gave out towels and stoked the furnaces of the bathhouses. There were special rooms built for each step of the bathing process. These included warm water (*tepidarium*), hot water (*caldarium*), and cold water (*frigidarium*). Some bathhouses had separate facilities for men and women. If that was not available, women visited the baths in the morning and men in the afternoon.

Ancient Romans did not use soap so slaves rubbed olive oil over bathers' bodies instead. The bather then entered the tepidarium for a soak in warm water to be followed by the caldarium for a steam bath. Slaves used a strigil (scraping tool) to take off the oil and dirt. The bathing ritual ended with a cold dip in the frigidarium and an application of scented oil. A patron could then request a massage or hair styling services.

Ancient Romans first used coins of bronze with engravings of a god or goddess on one side and a ship on the other. Molten metal was poured into a mold to make a circular disk. The hot blank disk was then pressed between two die with designs for the "heads" and "tails" sides of the coin. The stamp struck the die several times with a hammer. One such coin was a copper quadrans minted during the time of Emperor Augustus. Old coins were melted down and recycled into new money.

Augustus took control of the economy and supervised the minting of silver and gold coins. He allowed the provinces to control bronze and copper monies. Eventually, new coins were standardized to include fixed values. This system encouraged trade because the coins were accepted across the Empire.

When money became the standard for trading, merchants began using banks. These were located in the Roman Forum and were run by *equites* (businessmen) or freed slaves.

Q is for Quadrans
The Quadran had a heads and tails.
It was minted out of copper.
You'd spend one at the marketplace
if you were a Roman shopper.

Rr

Initially Rome was ruled by a succession of kings beginning with Romulus. By 509 BC the people were tired of harsh rulers. They overthrew Tarquinius and began a new kind of government. Referred to as the Roman Republic, it existed for almost five hundred years before the time of the emperors.

The Republic was important because it allowed the citizens the privilege of electing their officials. Two consuls were in charge of the senate and the army. The senate was a counseling body made up of the most important or wealthy *patricians* in Rome. By 82 BC, this group grew to six hundred senators!

Commoners (*plebeians*) did not participate in the government. They formed strikes and resorted to violence before things changed. At first, plebeians had a say in any laws they found unfair. Eventually they were allowed to run for office. The first plebeian consul was elected in 366 BC.

Julius Caesar was one of the most powerful leaders of the Republic era. He helped all of the people by making laws that encouraged equality regardless of whether they were rich or poor. Fearing that he held too much power, a group of senators stabbed Caesar to death in 44 BC. This action led to civil war and brought an end to the Republic.

R is for Republic

Rome flourished as a republic,
        this means people had a choice
as to who would be their leaders.
        Citizens were glad to have a voice.

Typically children went to a *ludus* (primary school) at the age of seven. The *Magister Lundi* (schoolmaster) conducted lessons in his house from before dawn to early afternoon. Pupils learned reading, writing, and arithmetic. At thirteen, most boys, and some girls, advanced to the *Grammaticus* where they acquired knowledge of history, astronomy, geometry, Roman and Greek literature, and music. Reciting the fables of the ancient Greek storyteller, Aesop, was a popular exercise.

Students used beads on a frame (*abacus*) to do math problems. Students wrote with a *stylus*, a type of pen, which was used to sketch onto a wax-covered wooden tablet. Some children used a reed dipped into wax made from soot to write on sheets of papyrus, a type of paper. Slaves constructed the books the students read by copying the well-known poetry and history of the ancient world. These items were considered great treasures. Soon libraries were built to house them. By the later empire, Rome had around thirty libraries.

At sixteen, wealthy Roman boys attended universities. Most of the centers were located in Greece. An important field of study was rhetoric taught by a *rhetor* who emphasized the art of public speaking. This meant speaking articulately as well as using persuasive questioning and debate skills.

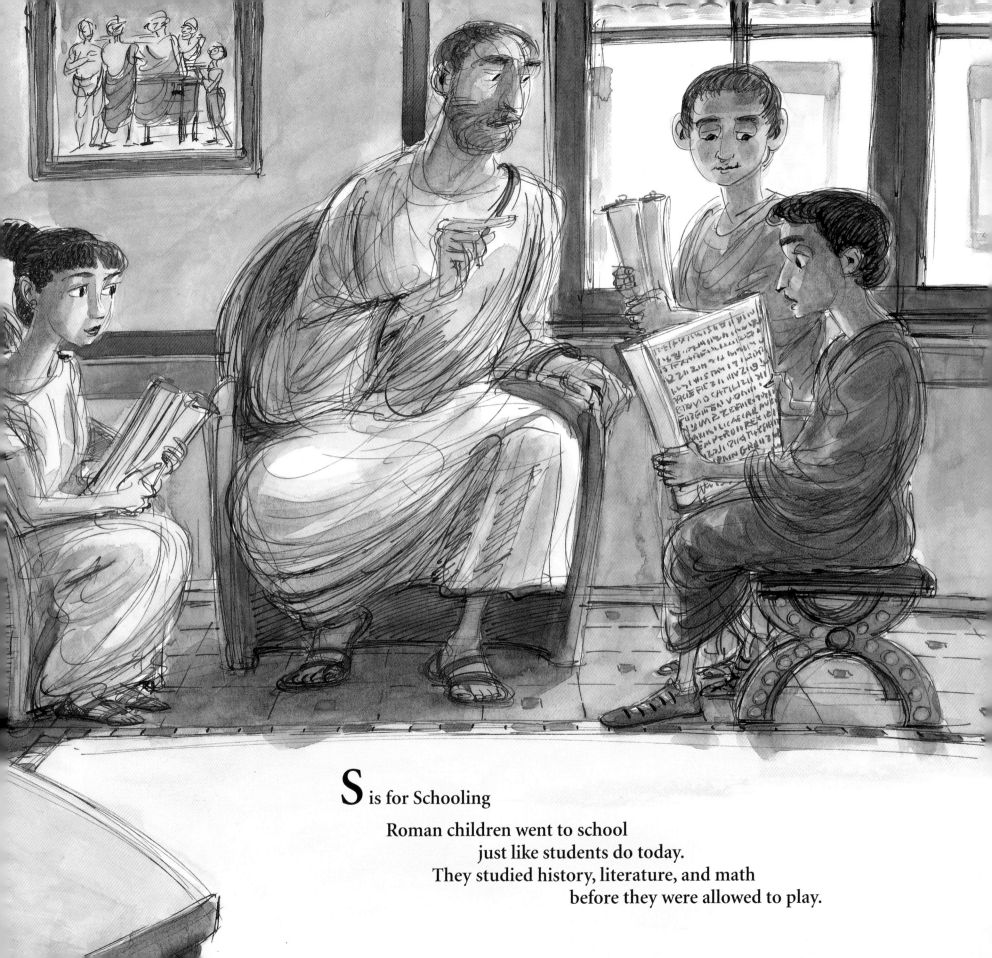

S is for Schooling

Roman children went to school
    just like students do today.
They studied history, literature, and math
        before they were allowed to play.

T t

T is for Temples
Romans built temples to honor gods
and show their appreciation
for all the good things in their lives,
and for the Roman nation.

The worshipping of many gods was most prominent during the time of the Empire. Architects built large imposing temples. These buildings were built to honor and provide a home for the gods that were thought to control the Roman people. Each temple included a shrine to a particular god or goddess and housed a sculpture of their image. These buildings also held treasures won through battle or donations from grateful patrons.

The Temple of Vesta (from the Greek word for "stove") can be found in the Roman Forum. Believed to contain an ancient fire brought by Aeneas, a prince of Troy who escaped to Italy, the temple was built in the shape of a primitive round hut with a hearth to symbolize the ever-lasting Roman State. It was not a traditional temple in the sense that it did not bear a sculpture of the goddess Vesta. Six handmaidens were entrusted with the job of keeping the fires of the hearth lit. These young women spent ten years in training, worked for another ten, and then spent a final ten years instructing the new inductees. If the fire was allowed to go out the maiden would be scourged, or whipped.

Between 27 and 25 BC the Roman general Marcus Agrippa built a temple to honor the seven gods of the planet. Called a *pan* (all) *theon* (of the gods), it burned to the ground several times. Emperor Hadrian ordered the reconstruction of the Pantheon around AD 120. He gave credit to Agrippa as can be seen by the engraved *portico*, or porch, leading to the entrance. This architectural wonder begins with eight Greek columns that hold a triangular-shaped structure called a *pediment*. Inside, a large dome, 142 feet (43 m) in diameter and the same distance from the floor to the top, is the center of the attraction. The concrete brick walls of the dome are 20 feet (6 m) thick at the base and less than 6 feet (2 m) on top. A hole or *oculus* at the top opens out to the sky.

The Pantheon is one of the largest single-span domes in the world and the oldest in Rome. Its guardianship passed to the popes of the Roman Catholic Church in AD 609. The church helped make it one of the best-preserved ancient buildings still in use today as a place of worship.

Roman towns were constructed in grids with straight streets that crossed at right angles. The blocks they formed were called *insulae* or "islands." Streets often covered the town's sewers and were paved in stone.

Rome was built on seven hills surrounding a swampy area. Draining this swampy basin began in the 8th century BC and resulted in a central meeting place. Called the *Forum Romanum,* Latin for open space or market, it was important to urban life. This was the gathering place for people to socialize, market, do business, or go to school. It was also where the government offices and religious temples were located.

Another important feature was the rostrum, or public speaking platform. *Orators,* public speakers, were encouraged to argue persuasively, and bystanders could stop and listen before going about their business.

At the height of the Empire, Rome had more than one million citizens. Many came to the Forum to hear the likes of Julius Caesar, witness lawmaking at the Senate, and visit one of the numerous shops. When the Christians came to power, the ancient Forum was neglected, buried, and used as cattle pasture. During the early part of the twentieth century, archaeologists unearthed this area and it is still being excavated today.

U u

U is for Urban Life

Urban life in ancient Rome
must have been exciting—
from market places to the Forum,
and gladiators fighting!

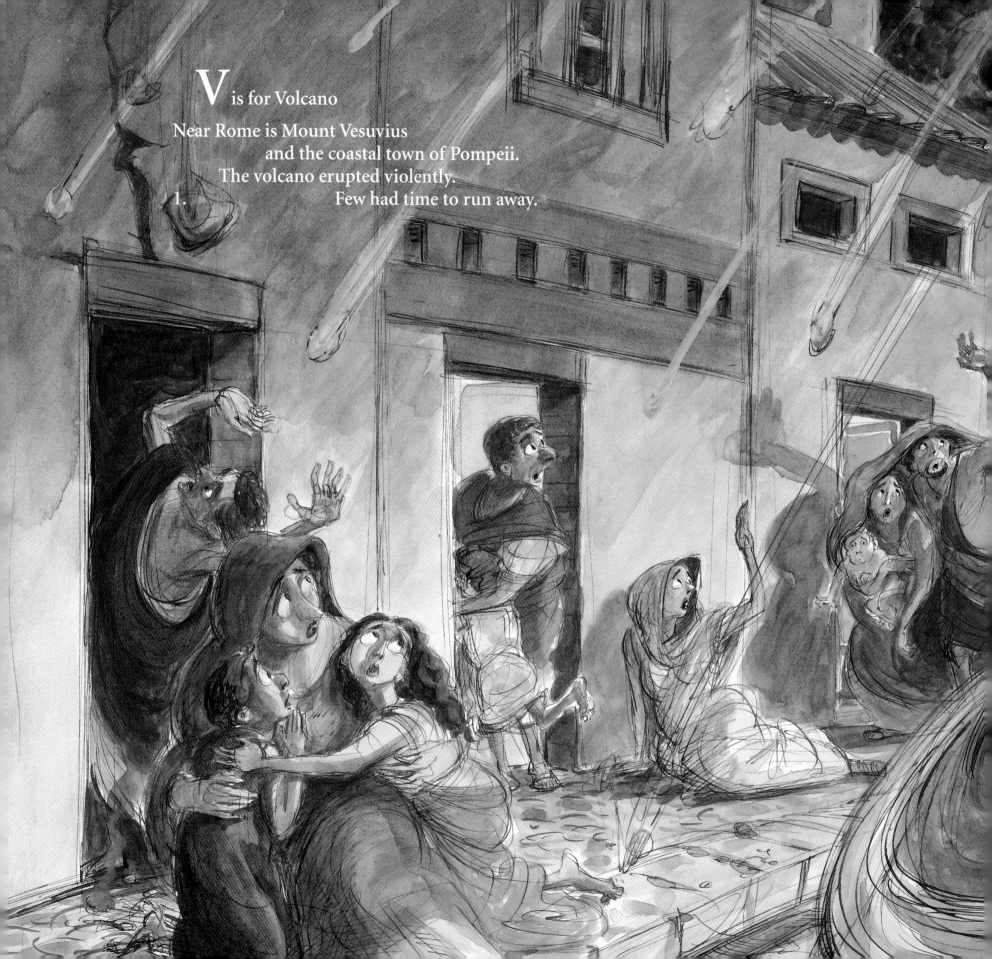

V is for Volcano

Near Rome is Mount Vesuvius
and the coastal town of Pompeii.
The volcano erupted violently.
Few had time to run away.

Southeast of Rome, near Mount Vesuvius, lies the town of Pompeii. The nearby volcano made the city susceptible to its eruptions. In AD 79 noxious fumes of sulfuric gas and molten debris from Vesuvius formed an ash cloud that suffocated most of its residents. Others died from the heat of the volcano or were crushed by falling buildings.

The cloud of ash and mud descended on the city, preserving it in amazing detail. The city was left like the day the volcano erupted. Petrified bread shows what kind of food had been baking when destruction came. Pumice from the volcano covered the bodies and formed casts that archaeologists filled with plaster to make sculptures of the citizens. Much of what is known about the ancient Roman way of life was discovered at Pompeii when excavations began in 1748.

Pliny the Younger, a famous writer who witnessed this horrible event, wrote: "Then we beheld the sea sucked back, and as it were repulsed by the convulsive motion of the earth; it is certain at least the shore was considerably enlarged, and now held many sea-animals captive on the dry sand. On the other side, a black and dreadful cloud bursting out in gusts of igneous serpentine vapour now and again yawned open to reveal long fantastic flames, resembling flashes of lightning but much larger."

V
v

A large city needs a constant supply of water for its inhabitants. Rome grew to a population of more than a million people because of plentiful water from the Tiber River, wells, and springs. However, with the demands for public baths, fountains, and toilets, even more water was required. Aqueducts solved this need as they channeled large volumes of water to Rome from faraway mountains.

The first aqueduct was built in 312 BC. It was a complex system of bridge-like structures made strong by arches. The aqueducts were elevated high above the ground to discourage stealing or poisoning of the water. Long stretches of open channels helped to send streams downhill toward towns across the Roman Empire. Wealthy people received their water through lead pipes that fed into their homes while the poor carried the precious liquid from public fountains. Eleven aqueducts supplied water to the Romans for drinking, cooking, and bathing.

In times of drought, Rome's first priority was public fountains. That is where most citizens received their water. Public baths were the first to have water cut off, followed by private houses.

W is for Water

Water moved through aqueducts
    built with stone, cement, and brick.
A system of arches and bridges
    worked well to do the trick.

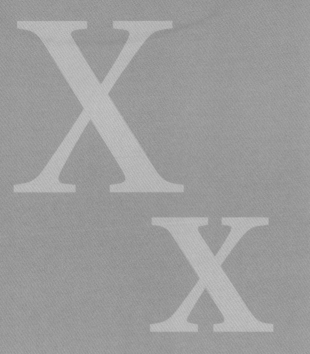

X is for Xerampelinae

Soldiers wore Xerampelinae,
        garments of bright blood red.
Usually made from natural fibers,
        such as linen or wool thread.

Xerampelinae is Latin for dark red garments. Roman garments were fashioned from large pieces of uncut cloth made of natural fibers like wool or linen, with few changes in style over thousands of years. Sewing was difficult so the clothing was pinned with a clasp or brooch (*fibula)* or tied by belts. Males wore a loincloth (which also served as bed clothes) and a short-sleeved, knee-length tunic. For public outings, a toga was placed over the tunic. Togas were large, semicircular sheets folded over the left shoulder and under the right and held in place by a fibula. A toga was heavy and difficult to arrange so, out of the public eye, gentlemen wore simple cloaks over tunics.

Women wore ankle-length tunics over which they placed a belted gown (*stola*) and often included a broad, colored cloak (*palla*). Jewelry and makeup complemented the garments. Women adorned themselves with necklaces, bracelets, rings, brooches, and hairpins made from precious metals, Spanish gold, and Asian jewels. Both men and women wore sandals at home and soft, animal-hide boots in public. The poor often went barefoot.

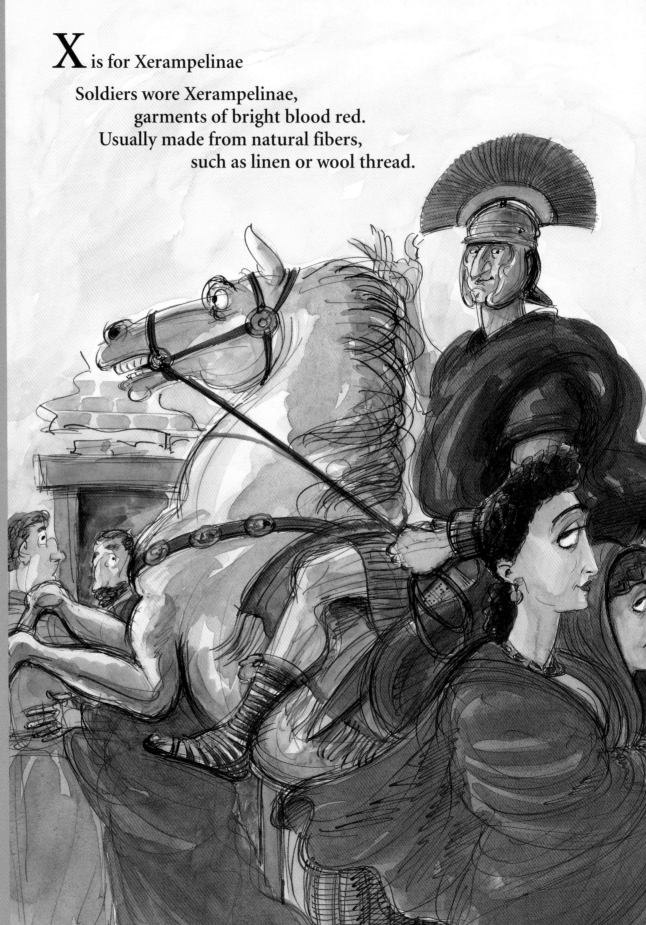

On the day a child was born the baby was presented to the father. If he received the child it signified acceptance. On the ninth day after birth, the child was named and given a charm (*bulla*) to help ward off evil.

Paintings and writings show that children played in ancient Rome much like today. Their toys and activities imitated the adults around them. Dolls, molded from clay or stuffed rags, were common. Young Roman children played with toy houses and carts. They enjoyed swings and seesaws and flew kites and played games with dice (*tali*). Knucklebones from sheep were used like jacks. Roman children also owned dogs, birds, monkeys, and cats as pets.

A child's first teacher was the parent and the first lessons were obedience. It was important to tell the truth and help others. Bedtime might be delayed when a guest was in the home so that the children could listen and learn.

Young boys were expected to fight in armor, throw a javelin, ride a horse, and box. Girls learned from their mothers how to run a household. A ceremony celebrated a boy's first beard followed by a trip to the barber and his first toga.

Y is for Youth

Roman youth were similar
to children of today.
They had chores to do at home,
but also liked to play.

Z is for Zama

The battle of Zama in Africa
ended a seventeen-year war.
The Romans defeated Hannibal,
something never done before.

Z z

Rome won many of its territories through battles, sometimes using its strong fleet of ships to enlarge the empire. They did this through a series of battles with Carthage in North Africa, called the Punic Wars. During the First Punic War (264 to 241 BC) Rome used its strong fleet of ships to enlarge its empire. The fleet defeated the army from Carthage, in North Africa, and gained control of the islands of Sicily, Corsica, and Sardinia.

During the Second Punic War beginning in 218 BC, a young Carthaginian military genius named Hannibal promised his father that he would avenge the losses of the First Punic War. Beginning with 100,000 troops and thirty-seven elephants Hannibal led his army over mountains and across rivers eventually entering Italy. Hannibal never reached Rome. The number of troops dwindled to forty-six thousand but he fought for the next sixteen years with no major defeats.

Rome then decided to meet the enemy on its own turf. The Roman soldiers attacked Spain and then Carthage eventually defeating Hannibal's army at Zama (northern Tunisia) in 202 BC. As a result, Rome obtained these areas as well as most of North Africa and became a major power in the Mediterranean.

Debbie and Michael Shoulders

Debbie is a full-time middle-school teacher and writes a weekly column called "Story Time" for Tennessee's oldest newspaper, where she reviews children's literature with an educator's slant. Mike has a doctorate of education, was an educator for 30 years, and now writes and travels year round across the US and Europe promoting his books and providing in-service training to teachers on literacy issues. He has written 10 books for Sleeping Bear Press. Mike and Debbie live in Clarksville, Tennessee.

Victor Juhasz

Victor Juhasz's previous books for Sleeping Bear include *R is for Rhyme*, *Z is for Zeus*, *Everyone Counts*, *H is for Honor*, and *D is for Democracy*. He serves on the board of the Society of Illustrators. His caricatures and illustrations appear regularly in many major magazines and newspapers including *Rolling Stone*, *Golf*, *Men's Journal*, *GQ*, *Opera News*, *Barron's*, and many others. Victor lives in Stephentown, New York.